ULTIMATE CARS

BMW

Rob Scott Colson

WAYLAND

Published in paperback in 2014 by Wayland
Copyright © Wayland 2014

Wayland
338 Euston Road
London NW1 3BH

Wayland Australia
Level 17/207 Kent Street
Sydney NSW 2000

Editor: Camilla Lloyd
Produced by Tall Tree Ltd
Editor, Tall Tree: Emma Marriott
Designer: Jonathan Vipond

British Library Cataloguing in Publication Data

Colson, Robert Scott.
  BMW. -- (Ultimate cars)
1. BMW automobiles--Juvenile literature.
  I. Title II. Series
  629.2'222-dc22

ISBN: 9780750281379

Printed in China

10 9 8 7 6 5 4 3 2 1

Wayland is a division of Hachette Children's
Books, an Hachette UK company.
www.hachette.co.uk

Contents

BMW

BMW (Bavarian Motor Works) is a car company based in Munich, Germany. The company began by making aircraft engines during World War I.

Banned from making aircraft after Germany lost the war, BMW changed to making motorcycles, which it still does today. The company started making cars in 1928. BMW now makes a range of cars that are high performance, which means that they reach very fast top speeds.

Amazing design

In 2004, BMW opened its new Virtual Reality Room. This advanced computer system allows engineers to handle new designs before they have been built. A visor enables them to look at a 3D image of a new engine part or control. Wearing special gloves, they experience what it would be like to operate the new part. In this way, they can better understand and even improve how it will work.

The 319/1, first made in 1935, was a stylish 2-seater convertible.

On the race track

BMW has raced its cars and motorcycles in motorsports since the 1930s. Drivers compete in Formula 1, the biggest competition for cars, with the team BMW Sauber, and they won their first race at the Canadian Grand Prix in 2008. The company also runs its own competition for young drivers called Formula BMW.

The BMW 328 was a sports car made between 1937 and 1939. It was driven in many races around Europe, and won the British RAC Rally in 1939.

Z4 Roadster

The Z4 Roadster is a 2-seater sports car that came into production in 2002. It has a very long bonnet that covers a powerful 3.2-litre engine, and the driver sits towards the back. This gives the car a very distinctive shape.

The Z4's shape ensures that weight is evenly distributed across all 4 wheels, which helps the car to accelerate very quickly. The Z4 can go so fast that BMW have limited its top speed to 250 kph.

Amazing design

A roadster – also known as a convertible – is a car with a soft roof that can be retracted (pulled back) in fine weather. The roof of the Z4 is operated electrically, and is one of the fastest retractable roofs in the world. At the push of a button, it pulls back in just 10 seconds to let the driver and passenger feel the wind in their hair.

steering wheel

gear paddle

gear stick

Smart gears

A car transfers the power of the engine to the wheels via the transmission, which has different gears. Low gears are used to accelerate or to drive uphill. High gears allow the car to reach its top speeds. The Z4's Sport Automatic gearbox allows the driver to change gear using either the gear stick or a paddle behind the steering wheel. If they prefer, they can also let the car change gears automatically.

STATS AND FACTS

YEARS OF PRODUCTION **2002–08**
ENGINE SIZE **3.2 litre**
NUMBER OF CYLINDERS **6**
TRANSMISSION **Manual/automatic**
GEARBOX **6-speed**
0–100 KPH (0–62 MPH) **5.7 seconds**
TOP SPEED **Limited to 250 kph**
WEIGHT (KG) **1385**
CO_2 EMISSIONS (G/KM) **292**
FUEL ECONOMY (L/100 KM) **8.6 (32.8 mpg)**

6 Series Coupé

The 6 Series is a 'grand tourer', which means that it is a sports car designed to drive long distances. It is larger and heavier than the Z4 Roadster, but with its enormous engine, it is just as exciting to drive.

A coupé has a hard roof that does not retract. The roof of a coupé helps to hold the car together, which improves its performance. This means that the 6 Series Coupé can accelerate from 0 to 100 kph half a second more quickly than the 6 Series Convertible.

The high-tech headrests save many a stiff neck. In the event of a crash, they move forwards to prevent the driver's or passenger's head from jerking backwards, which can cause a neck injury called whiplash.

Amazing design

The 6 Series Coupé is fitted with 'Night Vision', which uses infrared sensors to detect heat-producing objects, such as pedestrians or animals, up to 300 metres away. An image is displayed on the iDrive screen inside the car, so the driver knows someone is there before they can see them. This extra second might just save a life.

The iDrive screen shows information from the car's on-board computer.

Light but strong

To stand up to long journeys, a grand tourer needs to be strong and reliable. But adding strength also adds weight, which makes the car slower. The 6 Series Coupé's chassis (its 'skeleton') is made of high-tech material that is both strong and light. The roof is made of lightweight carbon fibre, which lowers the car's centre of gravity, making it easier to control at high speeds.

STATS AND FACTS

YEARS OF PRODUCTION **2007–present**
ENGINE SIZE **4.8 litre**
NUMBER OF CYLINDERS **8**
TRANSMISSION **Manual/automatic**
GEARBOX **6-speed**
0–100 KPH (0–62 MPH) **5.1 seconds**
TOP SPEED **Limited to 250 kph**
WEIGHT (KG) **1725**
CO$_2$ EMISSIONS (G/KM) **279**
FUEL ECONOMY (L/100 KM) **11.7**
(24.1 mpg)

M3

The M3 is a compact 4-seater designed for driving on roads and on the race track. It is very fast, and can accelerate from 0 to 100 kph in under 5 seconds.

The M3's engine is the key to its speed. The engine block – the heart of the engine in which the pistons pump up and down – is built by the same team that builds the engine block for the BMW Sauber Formula 1 car.

Amazing design

Four exhaust pipes pump the waste gas produced by the M3's engine out into the air. Car exhaust fumes are a major source of pollution, so each pipe is fitted with a device called a catalytic converter. The converters contain special chemicals known as catalysts. The catalysts react with the most harmful gases, such as carbon monoxide and nitrogen oxide, and turn them into safer gases such as carbon dioxide and nitrogen.

STATS AND FACTS

Years OF PRODUCTION **2005–present**
ENGINE SIZE **4 litre**
NUMBER OF CYLINDERS **8**
TRANSMISSION **Manual/automatic**
GEARBOX **6-speed**
0–100 KPH (0–62 MPH) **4.8 seconds**
TOP SPEED **Limited to 250 kph**
WEIGHT (KG) **1655**
CO_2 EMISSIONS (G/KM) **279**
FUEL ECONOMY (L/100 KM) **12.4 (22.8 mpg)**

Aerodynamic shape

As a car moves, it is slowed down by the air it is pushing against, known as air resistance. Every part of the M3 is designed to ensure that the air flows smoothly around it, reducing air resistance. Engineers test different shapes in wind tunnels to refine their aerodynamics (how they move through the air).

The backs of the M3's door mirrors are shaped to point into the wind and ease the air around them.

E23 7 Series

Launched in 1977, the E23 7 Series came equipped with the very latest gadgets.

E23 drivers were truly pampered: the most expensive models included heated seats, an electric sunroof and air-conditioning to keep them happy. With top speeds of over 200 kph, the E23 was no slouch, but its emphasis on comfort meant that it didn't quite match its faster high-performance cousins.

The Hydrogen 7 fuels up with liquid hydrogen at a special filling station.

Amazing design

In the early 1980s, BMW teamed up with the German Institute for Aviation and Space Flight to convert an E23 to run on liquid hydrogen rather than petrol. This was the start of a long-term project to find an alternative source of energy for cars. After 25 years of development work, BMW launched the first ever hydrogen-powered production car, the Hydrogen 7, in 2006.

STATS AND FACTS

YEARS OF PRODUCTION **1977–86 (this model 1981)**
ENGINE SIZE **3.4 litre**
NUMBER OF CYLINDERS **6**
TRANSMISSION **Manual**
GEARBOX **5-speed**
0–100 KPH (0–62 MPH) **7.3 seconds**
TOP SPEED **225 kph**
WEIGHT (KG) **1590**
CO_2 EMISSIONS (G/KM) **Not available**
FUEL ECONOMY (L/100 KM) **11 (25.7 mpg)**

New technology

The first 7 Series, which BMW codenamed the E23 Series, was fitted with the best technology of its time. This included a fuel-injected engine and an anti-lock braking system (ABS), which stops the wheels from locking while braking, preventing dangerous skids. These are standard features in cars today, but were rare in the 1970s.

507 Roadster

By the mid-1950s, BMW had lost its reputation as a manufacturer of fine 2-seater sports cars. The 507 Roadster was the model that would restore it.

The car's stylish, sleek shape was a hit among those who could afford it. Singer Elvis Presley bought one while he was serving in the US army in Germany.

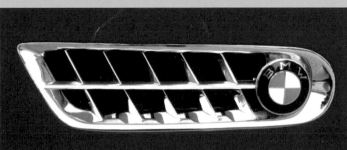

The 507's side air vents make the 507 instantly recognisable.

A costly car

Originally, BMW intended to make 5000 cars per year. But even though the 507 sold for several thousand pounds – many years' wages for the average worker – it cost even more to build, and each one lost BMW money. The 507 Roadster both restored BMW's reputation and drove it close to bankruptcy, and in the end only 252 cars were made. Remarkably, half a century later, over 200 are still on the road somewhere in the world.

Amazing design

The chassis for each 507 Roadster was modelled out of aluminium by hand, which means that no two are exactly the same. They came with an optional detachable hard top (roof), which was also made by hand, so that the hard top of one car would not fit any other.

STATS AND FACTS

Years of production **1956–59**
Engine size **3.2 litre**
Number of cylinders **8**
Transmission **Manual**
Gearbox **4-speed**
0–100 kph (0–62 mph) **11 seconds**
Top speed **196 kph**
Weight (kg) **1315**
CO_2 Emissions (g/km) **Not available**
Fuel economy (l/100 km) **11.8 (24 mpg)**

Formula 1 car

In 2006, BMW teamed up with Swiss company Sauber to compete in Formula 1, the biggest motorsports event of all.

Formula 1 cars must meet a strict set of rules. For example, the engine must have 8 cylinders, be no bigger than 2.4 litres, and cannot be turbo-charged. By limiting cars in this way, the race organisers ensure that teams have to come up with more efficient and competitive cars every year.

Amazing design

downshift (change to a lower gear)

screen displays information from the race marshals

upshift (change to a higher gear)

clutch paddle

The steering wheel is a Formula 1 driver's control centre. With both hands on the wheel, they can work the clutch, change gear, talk to their team and even take a drink. The wheel has a quick-release mechanism to allow the driver to climb out of the car in less than 5 seconds – which may save their life in a crash. This is driver Nick Heidfeld's wheel. The handles are made of silicon that has been moulded to the exact shape of his hands.

Pit stop

During a race, drivers come into the pits one or more times to change tyres and fuel up. The car is jacked off the ground, the wheels replaced, the tank filled with fuel, then lowered back down to rejoin the race. This is all done in under 10 seconds. Teams practise for many hours – a pit stop could be the difference between winning and losing.

STATS AND FACTS

YEARS OF PRODUCTION **2008**
ENGINE SIZE **2.4 litre**
NUMBER OF CYLINDERS **8**
TRANSMISSION **Semi-automatic**
GEARBOX **7-speed**
0–100 KPH (0–62 MPH) **2 seconds**
TOP SPEED **330 kph**
WEIGHT (KG) **605 (including driver)**
CO_2 EMISSIONS (G/KM) **Not available**
FUEL ECONOMY (L/100 KM) **217 (1.3 mpg)**

M1

The M1 was developed by BMW in collaboration with the Italian manufacturer Lamborghini. The car was designed to be driven in endurance races, in which cars drive as far as they can in a set number of hours.

Each M1 car was built by hand, and only 455 of them were ever made. Racing enthusiasts still race M1 cars today, decades after the last one drove off the production line.

Amazing design

To celebrate the 30th anniversary of the first M1, BMW designed the concept car M1 Homage. The design takes the M1's wedge shape and updates it using the latest technology to see what it would look like if it were made today. It has the M1's distinctive kidney-shaped twin grilles, which channel air over the front brakes to keep them cool.

STATS AND FACTS

YEARS OF PRODUCTION **1978–81**
ENGINE SIZE **3.6 litre**
NUMBER OF CYLINDERS **6**
TRANSMISSION **Manual**
GEARBOX **5-speed**
0–100 KPH (0–62 MPH) **5.5 seconds**
TOP SPEED **260 kph**
WEIGHT (KG) **1300**
CO_2 EMISSIONS (G/KM) **Not available**
FUEL ECONOMY (L/100 KM) **19.6 (14.4 mpg)**

Procar

In 1979 and 1980, BMW ran a series of races called the Procar Championship, in which drivers competed against each other in M1 cars. The Championship was a pure test of driver skill. Many Formula 1 drivers took part, including Niki Lauda and Nelson Piquet, who relished the opportunity of racing each other in identical cars.

BMW first asked an artist to paint their racing cars in 1975. The cars became known as the Art Cars. This is the M1 Art Car that competed in the 1979 Le Mans race. It was painted by the American artist Andy Warhol.

→Other racing

In addition to its Formula 1 team, BMW organises its own racing championship, known as Formula BMW.

Formula BMW is the first step up from karting in a young driver's career. Competitors as young as 15 can take part. BMW also enters cars in Touring Car championships, where production cars that have been adapted for racing drive against each other.

Formula BMW

In Formula BMW, all competitors drive the same single-seater FB02 car. Three separate series are held, in Europe, the Americas and Asia. The best drivers from these 3 regions then compete in the World Final. Promising drivers are given sponsorship to develop their skills, and each year's winner is invited to test drive for the BMW Sauber Formula 1 team. The Formula 1 star Sebastian Vettel started his career in this way.

Amazing design

BMW race the 320si in the World Touring Car Championship. A racing 320 looks different from one used for ordinary road driving. The chassis is the same, but the engine, suspension, brakes and wheels are all different. There is just one seat for the driver, who sits inside a specially built safety cage that gives extra protection in a crash.

steering wheel customised to suit the driver's height and arm length

head and neck support system

6-point safety belt straps driver firmly into their seat

STATS AND FACTS

FB02

YEARS OF PRODUCTION **2002**
ENGINE SIZE **1.2 litre**
NUMBER OF CYLINDERS **4**
TRANSMISSION **Semi-automatic**
GEARBOX **6-speed**
0–100 KPH (0–62 MPH) **4 seconds**
TOP SPEED **230 kph**
WEIGHT (KG) **526**
CO$_2$ EMISSIONS (G/KM) **Not available**
FUEL ECONOMY (L/100 KM) **Not available**

Glossary

aerodynamic
Shaped to minimise air resistance when moving at high speed.

air-conditioning
A system for controlling the temperature and humidity of the air inside the car.

carbon fibre
A lightweight man-made material often used instead of metal.

chassis
The frame or skeleton of the car to which the body and the engine are attached.

clutch
A means of disconnecting the engine from the wheels in order to change gear.

coupé
A car with a hard roof that cannot be removed.

endurance race
A race in which cars are driven as far as they can within a set time limit.

fuel economy
The rate at which a car uses fuel. It is measured in litres per 100 kilometres or miles per gallon.

fuel injection
A system that improves a car's performance by mixing fuel with air under high pressure as it enters the engine.

gear
A system of cogs that controls the transfer of power from the engine to the wheels. Low gears give extra power for acceleration or driving uphill. High gears are used for driving at faster speeds.

grand tourer
A sports car that is designed to be driven long distances.

handling
The ease with which a driver can control the car using the steering wheel.

karting
A form of racing using powered karts. Most racing drivers begin their careers in karting.

performance
A measurement of a car's power and handling. A car that accelerates quickly and has a high top speed is said to be high performance.

production car
A car built by a team of workers or robots, of which identical examples are made.

roadster
A car with a removable roof, also called a convertible.

transmission
The way in which a car transfers power from the engine to the wheels, via a gearbox that allows the driver to change gear.

Models at a glance

Model	Years Made	Numbers Built	Did You Know?
319/1	1934–36	178	A 319 could manage speeds of 130 kph with ease – not unusual today but very impressive in its time.
328	1937–39	464	One of the most successful sports cars of its day. In May 2008, a 328 sold in auction for £350,000.
507	1956–59	252	Elvis Presley owned a white 507 and gave it to James Bond film actress Ursula Andress in the 1960s.
E23 7 Series	1977–86	285,000	The first BMW model to be fitted with a 'check control' system, ABS and air-conditioning.
M1	1978–81	455	As one of BMW's rarer models, an M1 in good condition can fetch over £100,000 today.
Z4 Roadster	2002–08 (second generation in production from 2009)	200,000 per year	The Z4 Roadster has one of the fastest retractable roofs in the world.
M6	2003–present	Approximately 4,000 per year	With the speed limiter removed, an M6 could reach speeds of 330 kph.
M3	2005–present	Unknown. Limited by number of engines built	The E30 M3 has won more road races than any other BMW model in history.
320si	2005–present	2,600 per year	The engine has been hand built to a special design that reduces the number of moving parts.

Websites

www.bmw.co.uk

BMW's UK website, with features on all their current models, images to download and all the latest news.

www.autosport.com

A wealth of information about all forms of motorsport, including Formula 1 and touring cars.

www.bmw-motorsport.com

All the latest news from BMW's teams in Formula 1, touring cars and Formula BMW.

www.bmw-sauber-f1.com

Dedicated to the BMW Sauber Formula 1 team, with lots of exciting interactive features, such as a simulation of a wind tunnel test.

→Index